ANCIENT EGYPT

LAND OF THE PHARAOHS

for CHILDREN

by

John Richardson

Illustrated by

Robbie Peterson

Copyright

© 2023 John Richardson

All rights reserved. Nothing in this publication may be exhibited, copied, saved in an automated data file and/or made public, in any form or in any way, like by way of print, photocopy, microfilm recording device, or any other manner, without the prior consent of the author and the publisher. Please take note that according to copyright law, copyright protection lasts for the life of the author, plus 70 years. After that, it will be considered in the public domain. Therefore, all illustrations and pictures used in this book created over 70 years ago, are in the public domain. Illustrations and pictures used in this book created within 70 years were created by John S. Richardson unless stated otherwise. All text in this book has been written by John S. Richardson unless indicated as a quote.

ISBN 978-1-4467-5391-0

Dedication

To Rosemary, who shared my travels and adventures in Ancient Egypt, our two friends named Ola in Egypt, Carole and Stewart our children and my good friend and writer April.

The children in Ancient Egypt were cherished. This book is for children everywhere in the world to enjoy the history of the magical land of Mummies, Pharaohs and Pyramids.

Other publications by John Richardson
For children and adults:

The Romans and The Antonine Wall of Scotland
- ISBN 9-780244-502935

In Search of Agricola
- ISBN 9-781008-981669

Roman Britain for Children
- ISBN 9-781794-843196

Ancient Greece for Children
- ISBN 9-7814709-49259

Foreword

Thank you for reading my book. If you've enjoyed it, I would be most grateful if you would post a short review on Amazon. Your support does make a real difference, and I read all the reviews myself. Your feedback will help me improve my books.

Index

Introduction	06
The Lands of the Pharaohs	08
The River Nile floods	10
The Three Kingdoms	15
Valley of the Kings	18
How the Kings Ruled	19
Servants of the Pharaoh	21
Children in Egypt	24
Egyptian Army and Navy	27
Working in Ancient Egypt	31
Building in the past	34
Egyptian pyramids	35
Education in Ancient Egypt	37
Wearing clothes	39
Temples and Priests	41
Ancient tombs	43
The Afterlife and Mummies	45
The law in ancient Egypt	47
The gods and goddesses of ancient Egypt	49
The Sycamore Tree	51
The fruit bat	53
Glossary of words	55
Illustrations	56
Acknowledgment	57

Introduction

Hello, my name is Hori, and my sister's name is Meres Amun. We wish to tell you about the history of Ancient Egypt. Our father told us many stories. He said people came to Egypt some 5,000 years ago. Ancient Egypt is a very hot land to live in.

The Temples and the Gods were of great importance. Father told us that when the Pharaoh died, the temple Priests prepared the body into a mummy. Sometimes, they buried the Kings inside large tombs built underground.

But we also had time to play and enjoy games and had lots of fun with our friends. We had to be very careful if we went swimming in the Nile because of the crocodiles.

Father told us the River Nile was important for the prosperity of Egypt. We also have school. Parents with enough money would get a teacher to teach us to write and read.

Hori: *"When did people come to Egypt?"*

Hello, my name is Hori

The lands of the Pharaohs

Did you know that the largest part of Egypt was made up of desert sands, making it seem empty and barren? There were also large rocks and high cliffs. The river Nile made Egypt a place where people could live and work. It created a vast green area with trees and vegetation. The people called it "The beloved land", and it gave Egypt its wealth and was good for agriculture.

When the Egyptians wanted good wood for building homes, they had to bring this wood from other countries. The native trees along the Nile, like palm and tamarisk, were not suitable. But the Nile also gave the people mud and reed plants, which they could use to make mud bricks. They also used stones from the desert for building.

People made jewellery from semi-precious stones and gold. Egypt had copper but no iron, which put them at a disadvantage when making tools and arms.

Hori: *"Can you name two native Egyptian trees?"*

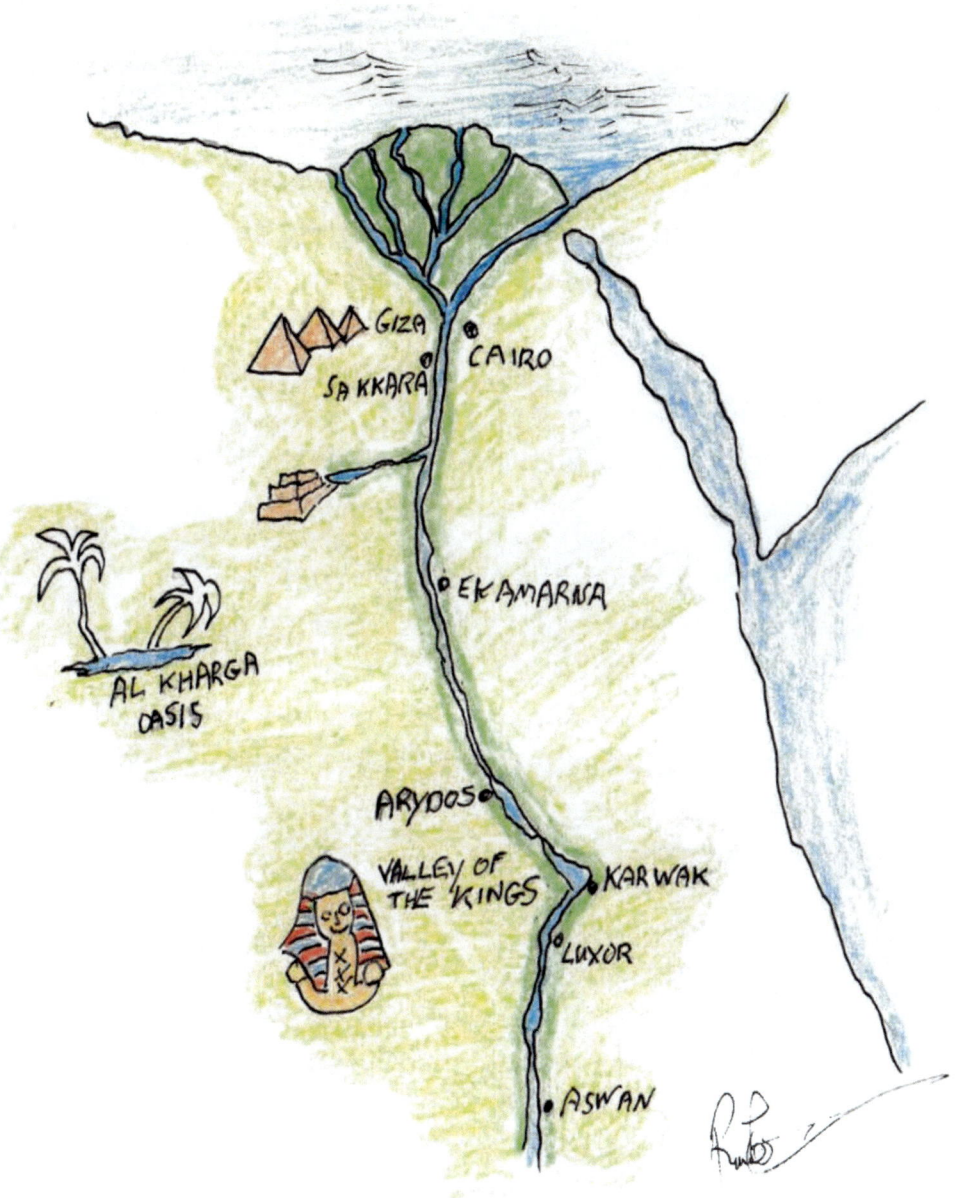

Map of Egypt

The River Nile floods

There were two rivers which formed the Nile. The Blue Nile ascended from the mountains in Abyssinia, and the White Nile from the waters in central Africa. Today, the city of Khartoum stands where those two rivers came together. From there, the Nile made its way north towards the Mediterranean Sea.

In Ancient Egypt, the Nile had its annual floods called the Inundation. These occurred from July to September. It was a joyous time for the people of Egypt and their farmers as it brought rich mud and water to their fields. Years with few floods limited the growth of crops and caused starvation.

On the other hand, too much flooding could wash houses and crops away. Dykes were built to prevent flooding but also channelled water to the fields. The Pharaoh ordered the use of *Nilometres*, gauges that showed the water level of the Nile.

The farmers called flooded land covered with river mud *The Black Land*. The desert was called *The Red Land*.

Hori: *"Can you name the Gauge used to measure water levels?"*

The Blue Nile

The Nilometres

Amenhotep VI ruled in Ancient Egypt from BC 1379 to 1362 BC. He started a new religion in Egypt and worshipped the Sun, named the Aten.

He also changed his name to Akhenaten. He abandoned the old Gods of Egypt and moved from the city of Thebes to a new city he built, which he named Tel-el-Amarna.

He married a very beautiful lady called Nefertiti, and they had six children. When he died, the priests and the people quickly left this new capital, returned to Thebes, and worshipped the old gods as before.

Slowly, this abandoned city disappeared into the sands until its ruins were discovered.

Hori: *"Who was Nefertiti"*

Nile Floods

The Three Kingdoms

Egypt had three Kingdoms. The Old Kingdom existed from 2640 to 2130 BC. This was the period when the first pyramids were built, and many other prominent buildings were constructed. It was also a flourishing time for the arts, medicine, literature and science. The Old Kingdom was hardly involved in war and enjoyed peace and prosperity. The soldiers kept all the people safe and patrolled the borders and frontiers. People could participate in trade safely and were very prosperous.

The Middle Kingdom existed from circa 2030 to 1650 BC. The country was ruled by the Pharaoh and powerful Governors, who carried out much of the Royal Powers. It was also the time of the Royal Dynasties XI-XIIII in Egypt. Slowly, however, the Pharaohs took back much of the powers from the Governors. A land to the south of Egypt, Nubia, was invaded, and the frontier moved further south.

The New Kingdom existed from 1550 to 1070 BC. This period met with war and turmoil when the Hyksos invaded Egypt. By 1567 BC, a new powerful Princes defeated the Hyksos and drove them from the land. This was a time of brilliant warrior Kings (Pharaohs). Tribute and recognition poured into Egypt from its expanded empire and beyond.

Prominent temples and tombs were built in Egypt. One of Egypt's greatest Kings was Thutmose III, and his ambassadors made important treaties with surrounding and faraway lands.

Hori: *"How many Kingdoms were there in Ancient Egypt?"*

The Nile

Valley of the Kings

The Valley of the Kings has the Tombs and Graves of many of the Kings of Ancient Egypt. They were built for the Kings (Pharaohs) who ruled in Ancient Egypt.

By 1000 BC, they had stopped using pyramids as the King's tombs. Instead, they built secret burial tombs for the Kings. They believed they would be safer from Tomb robbers. To date, more than 60 tombs have been found in the Valley of the Kings.

These tombs were built by workers and skilled artisans deep into the sides of the hills and with many large chambers connected with corridors. The walls and many of the ceilings were covered with beautiful paintings of the Kings, Gods and Goddesses, as well as the ancient Hieroglyphics.

One of the longest tombs found was of the famous Queen named Hatshepsut. This Queen had a renowned Architect named Senmut, who had a funeral temple built for her at Thebes called Deir-el-Bahari. One of the children of Hatshepsut grew up to become Tuthmosis III, a well-known warrior king.

After 1000 BC, many of the tombs were emptied by the Royal Priests. The mummies were removed and buried in other secret places in the Valley of the Kings to stop robbers from stealing the Royal Treasures.

Hori: *"What was the name of the famous Queen?"*

How the Kings ruled

Initially, Ancient Egypt was split into two kingdoms: The Lower and Upper Kingdoms. As the name says, they were both ruled by a king. However, in time, the two merged and became one kingdom. But there were still two crowns; the King held what was called a double crown. The King, or rather, Pharaoh, lived in a palace called The Great House.

The people of Egypt believed he was the God called Horus who lived on earth to rule Egypt. The Pharaoh had more than one wife, and his Queen was called *The Great Wife*.

Most Kings were men, but one famous Queen was called Hatshepsut. She officially became "King" and ruled Egypt successfully, and the Egyptians built a great temple honouring her at Thebes.

Another King, Amenhotep IV, ruled Egypt from ca 1380 to 1363 BC. He abandoned the Gods popular with the people and worshipped a new sun God instead. This God was called Aten.

Amenhotep's rule was not successful, and when he died, the Priests and the people returned to their old Gods. His wife was called Nefertiti, and they had six children. Nefertiti was known for her beauty. The Ancient Egyptians thought the King came as a child from the Gods in heaven.

Next to being King, he also worked as the High Priest and spoke for all the Gods and Goddesses in Egypt.

Hori: *"Who was the Queen who became a King?"*

How the Kings Ruled

Servants of the Pharaoh

To enable the Pharaoh to manage Egypt, people were employed to act on his behalf. The Pharaohs hired deputies who were named Viziers. There was one for Lower Egypt and one for Upper Egypt. They employed staff to look after the Treasury and state offices.

They did not use money but got paid with both goods and food. Goods and food were kept in royal storehouses and guarded by soldiers to prevent theft. Some goods and minerals were not found in Egypt. Officials from each district in the land search for them outside of Egypt.

In Egypt, every person served the King and worked in many different ways for him. To administrate this and keep track of things, the state had to employ hundreds of scribes. From their records, we learned a lot about Egypt.

Hori: *"What were the Pharaoh's deputies called?"*

Hatshepsut, the first Queen of Egypt

Amenhotep IV

Children in Egypt

In Ancient Egypt, boys were thought to misbehave and needed discipline. It would make them better at dealing with work later in life. Girls had to obey their parents but had an easier time.

All children learned about the Egyptian Gods and Goddesses. Parents also told them to keep their hearts pure and help others with good deeds. If people could not have children, they were encouraged to adopt them.

From the age of 5, all children had to learn. Girls and boys were encouraged to play games that made them agile and strong. Girls had to learn to care for other children and were given dolls which were made to look lifelike.

Children were given charms and amulets for protection. Nevertheless, many young children died of diseases. Children with wealthy parents were taught reading, writing and other wisdom. Ordinary children were taught skills and crafts.

When children reached the age of 12 to 15, they were seen as young adults.

Hori: *"What was the age children had to start to learn?"*

Children in Egypt: Hori and his sister Meresamun

Children in Egypt

Egyptian Army and Navy

The Army in Ancient Egypt constantly changed its appearance. The soldiers were mainly in the form of infantry. But when a warlike people called the Hyksos invaded Egypt, they brought their horses and chariots.

The Egyptians learned quickly and adopted the use of chariots and horses. By the time of the New Kingdom, the Army had four divisions named after the Gods Amum, Re, Ptah and Sutekh. They all had their standards, flags and trumpets.

The soldiers' main weapons were the bow and arrows, spears, swords, and clubs. Also, by this period, soldiers wore armour and helmets.

The Egyptian Navy had a history that was almost the same length of time as Egypt. The early ships of the Egyptian Navy sailed the Nile River and were made from reeds. Ships used on the seas were made from cedar wood, which came from what is now known as Lebanon.

Soldiers of the Egyptian Army

During the time of Thutmose III, they defended Egypt against the enemy they called the Sea People. But they also carried food and supplies to the forts along the Nile.

During the reigns of the Pharaohs Thutmosis III and Rameses, the Navy became of great importance. The Kings knew that having ships that were both fast and could carry supplies and communications was necessary. Thutmosis III also built a port and dockyard for shipbuilding and repairs at Memphis.

The Navy needed reliable ships to carry the soldiers serving in the Egyptian Army with supplies to where these were needed. During the time of the New Kingdom, the Kings of Ancient Egypt realised that for Egypt to be powerful and be able to defend itself, it would need a powerful and strong Navy.

Hori: " *How many Army divisions were there, and what kind of wood was used for building the ships?*"

The Egyptian Navy

Working in Ancient Egypt

Farming was one of the primary professions. The season would start in October. By that time, the flood waters of the Nile had passed. The ground was waterlogged, and they used ploughs to help them cultivate the soil. The ploughs were pulled by oxen. The farmer operated and followed the plough and threw the seeds into the soil. Then followed a busy time keeping weeds down and watering the soil until the new crops were ready to be harvested. In the field, they grew mainly barley and wheat, but they also grew fruits and different vegetables. The harvest was in or around April. Good pasture land was scarce because of the lack of rain. The Ancient Egyptians raised goats, sheep and cattle. They also had plenty of fish and birds, which they trapped in their nets along the Nile. Together, this made for a balanced diet. One of their most popular drinks was beer and wine. Food and drink were sweetened with honey from the bees they kept.

Hori: *"What were the animals that pulled the ploughs?"*

Farming and working in Egypt

Building in the past

Many of the Egyptian houses or large palaces were built using mud bricks. Mud bricks were easily made from straw and mud. But when building elaborate tombs and temples, they used longer-lasting materials like stone. They believed stones would last forever.

The work was done by professional stonemasons and skilled brickmakers. To build the large temples and tombs, they needed hundreds of workers.

During the times of the New Kingdom, there were many prisoners of war whom the Pharaohs used as slaves who were involved in all the building projects.

Hori: *"What material was used to build the tombs and temples?"*

Building in Egypt

Egyptian pyramids

The Ancient Egyptians built many pyramids during the time known as the Fourth Dynasty, nearly 4000 years ago. They were then, and today, seen as wonders of the world.

Their purpose was to serve as burial monuments for the dead Kings and safely guard the gold and goods placed close to them for the Afterlife. Because Egypt is a very hot land with a dry climate, there was very little decay to the stones and the goods inside them.

The pyramids were built on the sands at Giza. Smaller pyramids were built for the families and lower officials of the King.

When they built these vast monuments, the craftsmen and workmen used nearly six million tons of Limestone to construct the pyramids.

These enormous blocks of stone were placed on sledges and pulled by Oxen or men. The first pyramids were step-shaped in appearance, but as the Egyptians' skills developed, they were able to build smooth-sided pyramids.

The bright sunlight made the pyramids appear to the people as almost illuminating lights in the desert. The tops of the pyramids could have been finished with highly polished stones to enhance the reflection of light even more.

The pyramids had four sides, and they required the artisans to have a good knowledge of science and maths to build them.

These monuments of the past can still be seen today, thousands of years later, at Giza in Egypt.

Hori: *"How many tons of stone were used in building a pyramid?"*

Education in Ancient Egypt

After the two Kingdoms joined together, writing began to appear. This took the form of signs and drawings, which we call hieroglyphics. When we grew up, it was most important that we could both read and write. This meant that we could have a promising career. All government business and religious work in the temples required those skills.

Rich people would employ teachers for their children and send them to the best temples and priests to teach them. Less wealthy parents would hire a local priest to help with their children's education.

Teaching began by copying stories and written words from the past, known as the wisdom texts. Some temples would also have schools to train scribes.

Becoming a scribe would be very rewarding and open many doors. The rich would also have their children taught mathematics, history, music and languages.

Teaching children began when they were five years old.

Hori: *"What age could children begin to be taught?"*

Education in Egypt

Wearing clothes

Because Egypt was so hot, most of the clothes that were worn were made from linen. Other available materials were wool and leather. Due to the heat, most garments were quite simple in design.

The women liked to wear fitting dresses, which had wide straps to hold them up over their shoulders. Men wore mainly skirts that came down to their knees or sometimes their ankles. These skirts were worn with a leather or linen belt. In the colder winter months, cloaks made from wool were worn to keep them warm.

Women also wore thinner drapes over their dresses. Paintings from the tombs showed that rich people could afford more expensive clothes. The poorer Egyptians were not able to afford these fine linens, so they wore cheaper fabrics that were often coarse.

Most people preferred white fabrics, which reflected the heat. But they also wore garments that had many colours and patterns.

Hori: "What material were most of the clothes made from?"

Clothes in Egypt

Temples and priests

Egyptians believed the Gods and Goddesses lived in their dedicated temples. It was where people went to worship the various Gods at their shrines. Temples were built like houses with three main spaces.

The first was an open courtyard where people passed large pylons known as gateways. This was where much of the business was carried out. Ordinary people could not go further inside the temple.

The second room was filled with large stone pillars called a hypostyle. It was only the priests and priestesses that could go into this hall. The third room was where the Gods and their statues were. This was the inner sanctum of the Gods.

Some temples had a sacred lake where the priests and priestesses did their divine worship on water. One of those temples was the temple at Karnak. The temples employed many people, and trades-people were always nearby. These included craftsmen, scribes, musicians, dancers and slaves.

Hori: *"How many spaces were inside the temple?"*

Temples, Gods and Goddesses

Ancient tombs

Early Egyptians buried their relatives who passed away in a simple grave. They just dug holes in the hot sands and covered them with stones to protect against wild animals and the weather.

As they developed their building skills, they started building tombs from mud bricks called *mastabas*. The wealthy and nobles built wonderfully decorated tombs, while the Pharaohs built large tombs and pyramids.

The first pyramids were built like steps but later with smooth lines, like at Giza. By the time of the New Kingdom, they also cut tombs out of solid rock. Most of these are on the West Bank, close to Thebes.

When a King died, a long procession of priests, dancers and singers went with him to his grave. Inside the tombs, the priests placed everything that needed to continue to live in the next world. Prayers and spells secured safe passage to the God Osiris, who guarded the Afterlife.

Hori: "What was the name of the God who guarded the afterlife?"

Ancient Tombs in Egypt

The Afterlife and Mummies

The Egyptians believed that after you died, you lived again in the Afterlife. The Afterlife was called the *Land of Two Fields*, where you lived and played again. However, you could not simply just go there. Food and goods had to be collected and placed with the bodies in the graves. These helped them live happily in the Afterlife.

Clay models were made of little people who could do magic work to help them on the other side. The deceased's name was written on a *cartouche* and placed in the coffin.

Poor people laid their relatives in the hot sands, while wealthy people paid Priests to make their bodies into Mummies. The body was dried and preserved and wrapped up in bandages.

Then you had to be brave as your heart was weighed in the *Hall of Maat* to see if you had been telling the truth and were a good person. Egyptians also believed the soul and the body were in two parts and called the Ba and the Ka.

Hori: *"What was the name of the land of the Afterlife?"*

Funny Mummy

The law in Ancient Egypt

When Egyptians had a dispute, they took their case to the lower court. Cases not settled in the lower court were taken to a higher court, which had a Vizier as a judge.

People did not go to the court of the Vizier unless their case was serious. He tried his best to be fair, but you also had to show your evidence. If you did not have a good case, you could end up in more trouble. There was an even higher court where the King judged.

Another way of getting justice was from the Goddess Maat. She also dealt with justice, and her priests said what was either right or wrong. Each town had its courts in which the elders gave their verdicts.

If women broke the law, they were treated the same as men. Everyone had to defend themselves as there were no lawyers yet. If you were found to be guilty of a serious crime, you and your family could be exiled.

Hori: *"What was the higher court judge called?"*

The Law in Ancient Egypt: Exile

The Gods and Goddesses of Ancient Egypt

Ra was known as the great sun god but also had other names given by the Ancient Egyptians. He ruled during the Old Kingdom.

Khepri was known as the young sun god and was shown as a blue scarab beetle.

Osiris was the son of Ra and also became a king. Osiris ruled in the underworld. He wore a white crown and held in his hands a crook and a fail.

Horus was the son of Osiris. Many Ancient Egyptians believed that all the Pharaohs descended from the God Horus. He also inherited the royal throne.

Amun became the Sun God during the time of the New Kingdom and, like RA, the supreme ruler.

Isis was one of the most important Goddesses, the wife of the God Osiris and the mother of Horus. Isis gave comfort to the deceased. Isis helped people with their need for magic and spells.

Hathor was worshipped in Ancient Egypt as the Goddess of motherhood and fertility and helped women during childbirth. She enjoyed both dance and music.

Bast was the daughter of the Sun God Ra and was shown as having the head of a Cat and the body of a woman. The large temple dedicated to her was named Bubastis.

Hori: *"What was the name of the Beetle Scarab God?"*

Ra God of Gods

The Sycamore Tree

The Sycamore tree was found in Upper and Lower Egypt and also in the many Oases. It was one of the most important trees and gave the Egyptian people fruit.

The Goddess Nut was associated with this tree. Remains of the Sycamore tree have been found in Ancient Egypt, dating back to 3000 BC. The Sycamore trees were very large, and the Egyptians made coffins from its wood. They also used it to make other wooden goods, including toys for the children.

The Sycamore was also known as the Fig Tree of the Pharaoh. It also grew in Ancient Israel. The Egyptians found that it was healthy to eat the figs from the tree and that the leaves made a tea good for healing. The sap of the Sycamore tree was used to make sweet syrup. This amazing tree was a true gift to the people of Ancient Egypt.

Hori: *"What did the Egyptians make from the leaves of the Sycamore tree?"*

Sycamore Tree

The fruit bat

In Egypt, there were many different species of Bats. One of them was called the Fruit Bat because it loved to eat any fruit. They were considered by some to be pests, but everyone knew they were good pollinators.

In Ancient Egypt, bats were quite common, and they could be found living in many parts as well as along the river Nile. They even lived in the deserts and up in the north in the delta. All kinds of Bats, including the Fruit Bat, could be found living in tombs, temples, caves and the Pyramids, as well as in people's houses.

If they found a deserted building, they would stay inside in large numbers. People in Egypt thought that bats were just another kind of bird, as both had wings and could fly.

In some cases, when people died, they would have a bat and an owl placed in their mummy coffin. They believed those would help them fly from the darkness to the light of heaven.

Egyptians also wore amulets showing bats to protect them from evil spirits.

Hori: *"In what kind of buildings did bats live?"*

Egyptian Fruit Bat

Glossary of words

Here are some words used in this book that you may wish to learn about:

- Priests and Priestesses were people who worked in the temples where they worshipped the many Gods and Goddesses.
- Mummies were the bodies of people who had died. Special priests would prepare their bodies for the next life.
- Temples were places Egyptian people went to offer prayers and worship the gods and the dead Pharaohs.
- Tombs were buildings where the dead were put in a coffin and then buried either in the ground or in tombs carved in rock.
- Viziers were head administrators to the Pharaoh and had the power to give justice in the name of the King in the courts.
- Pharaohs were Egyptian kings.
- Hieroglyphs were Egyptian writings that looked like pictures and symbols. It allowed them to write down stories and keep records.
- Scribes were writers, trained from an early age to study and know how to write and draw hieroglyphs.

Illustrations

Robbie Peterson created the illustrations in this book.

Hori: *"Can you tell me which illustration in the book you liked best?"*

Acknowledgement

To all the children in the entire world.

To all members past and present and fans of the Roman Living History Society The Antonine Guard, which promotes the history of the Ancient World.

Permitte Divis Cetera

Printed and bound by CPI Group (UK) Ltd, Croydon, CR0 4YY
23/11/2023
03590754-0001